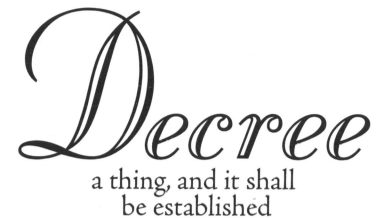

Decree

a thing, and it shall be established

J O B   2 2 : 2 8

THIRD EDITION

Decree

a thing, and it shall
be established

JOB 22:28

THIRD EDITION

Patricia King

Published by XP Publishing
P. O. Box 1017
Maricopa, Arizona 85139
XPpublishing.com

ISBN: 978-1-936101-81-8

Contents

Introduction..7

Prayer of Dedication...9

Praise and Worship..11

Everlasting Love..13

Who I Am in Christ..15

Blessing...21

Favor...25

Victory...27

Wisdom..31

Glory...35

Provision and Resource......................................39

Christian Character..43

Spiritual Strength..47

Empowered to Go..51

Health and Healing..55

Business, Ministry, and Workplace.......................59

Family and Children..61

Great Grace..65

Rejuvenation...69

I Am Supernatural in Christ................................73

12 Decrees for Your Nation.................................77

Power of Prayer...81

My Prayer List...82

Personal Decrees..86

Introduction

$\mathcal{T}$he powerful Word of God is well able to profoundly influence your life. In Christ you have an eternal and unbreakable covenant. All of His promises are "*Yes*" and "*Amen*" (2 Corinthians 1:20) to you! Daily confession of the Word will strengthen your inner man and prepare you for every good work. The following are some reasons why the confession of the Word is found to be powerful in our lives.

The Word of God:

+ Is eternal in the heavens – *Matthew 24:35*
+ Will not return void – *Isaiah 55:11*
+ Frames the will of God – *Hebrews 11:3*
+ Dispatches angels – *Psalm 103:20*
+ Brings light into darkness – *Psalm 119:130*
+ Is a lamp unto our feet and a light unto our path – *Psalm 119:105*
+ Secures blessings – *Ephesians 1:3; 2 Peter 1:3*

- Is seed – *Mark 4*
- Is our weapon of warfare – *Ephesians 6:10-20; 2 Corinthians 10:3-5*
- Pulls down mindsets – *2 Corinthians 10:3-5*
- Creates – *Romans 4:17*
- Sanctifies – *John 17:17*
- Strengthens the spirit man – *Ephesians 5:26*
- Ensures answers to prayer – *John 15:7*

May you truly enjoy a season of strengthening and may you be forever established in the manifestation of His glorious Word.

In His victorious service with you,

Patricia King

Prayer of Dedication

I dedicate myself to You this day in spirit, soul and body. Convict me of any ways in my thoughts, words or deeds that have been displeasing to You. I ask for cleansing from all sin according to Your Word that promises that if I confess my sin, then You will be faithful to forgive me and to cleanse me from all unrighteousness.

As I confess and decree Your Word, may Your Holy Spirit help me to be a passionate worshipper, a lover of truth, and a faithful child who brings pleasure to Your righteous heart.

May I experience spiritual strengthening through the power of Your Word, for Your Word does not return void but accomplishes everything it is sent to do.

Grant unto me a spirit of wisdom and of revelation in the knowledge of Christ for the glory of Your Name and Kingdom.

In Jesus' name, I pray. AMEN

With my whole heart I have sought You;
Oh, let me not wander from Your commandments!
Your word I have hidden in my heart,
That I might not sin against You.
— Psalm 119:10-11 —

Praise and Worship

*H*eavenly Father, I worship You in spirit and in truth. Along with the host of heaven, I declare:

Holy, holy, holy, Lord God Almighty,
Who was and is and is to come!
You are worthy, O Lord, to receive glory and honor
and power;
For You created all things, and by Your will they exist.
Blessing and honor and glory and power
Be to Him who sits on the throne,
And to the Lamb, forever and ever!
Holy, holy, holy is the Lord of hosts;
The whole earth is full of His glory!

– Revelation 4:8,11; 5:13; Isaiah 6:3

You, O Lord, are sitting on Your throne, high and lifted up, and the train of Your robe fills the temple. I ascribe greatness to You, for You are my God and my Rock. Your work is perfect, and all Your ways are just. You are a God of faithfulness and without injustice; righteous and upright are You.

I love You, O Lord my God, with all my heart, mind and strength. You are the Lord, and there is no other. There is no God besides You. I glory in Your holy name, and my heart rejoices in You. I will seek Your face evermore! I bless You, O Lord, my God. You are very great. You are clothed with honor and majesty.

While I live, I will praise You. I will sing praises to You while I have my being. The high praises of God will be in my mouth and a two-edged sword in my hand.

> *Praise the Lord!*
> *Praise the Lord from the heavens;*
> *Praise Him in the heights!*
> *Praise Him, all His angels;*
> *Praise Him, all His hosts!*
> *Praise Him, sun and moon;*
> *Praise Him, all you stars of light!*
> *Praise Him, you heavens of heavens,*
> *And you waters above the heavens!*
> *– Psalm 148:1-4*

Scriptural References:
Deuteronomy 32:3-4; Psalm 104:1; 105:3-4; 146:2; 149:6; Isaiah 6:1; 45:5; John 4:24

Everlasting Love

The Lord loves me with an everlasting love and has promised to give me a future and a hope. With loving-kindness He has drawn me unto Himself. I look carefully and intently at the manner of love the Father has poured out upon me. It is through this love that He has called me to be His dear child. I am completely and fully accepted in Him, my God and Savior.

Nothing can separate me from the love of God that is in Christ Jesus my Lord – not tribulation or distress, not persecution, famine or nakedness; not peril, sword, angels, principalities, powers; death, nor life; neither things present nor things to come – absolutely nothing can separate me from the love of God which is in Christ Jesus my Lord.

God's love towards me is patient and kind. His love for me bears all things, believes all things, hopes all things and endures all things. His love will never fail. His love for me is so rich that He gave His only begotten Son.

Because of this, I will never perish but will have everlasting life with Him. As a result of God's great love for me, I have an unbreakable, eternal covenant with Him. Through this covenant of love, He has put His laws within my heart and has written His commandments upon my mind.

I have been invited to the Lord's banqueting table and His banner over me is love! His love is better than the choicest of wines. Through His intimate love, He draws and invites me to follow after Him. I am fair and pleasant unto Him. I am rooted and grounded in His love and am well able to comprehend with all believers what is the width and length and depth and height of His unfailing love. I have been called to know this rich love that surpasses knowledge so that I may be filled with all the fullness of God. I truly am the object of His deepest love and affection!

Christ's perfect love has cast out fear in me and has enabled me to be a passionate lover of God and others. Love is my greatest aim in life.

Scriptural References:
Song of Solomon 1:2,4; 2:4; Jeremiah 31:3; Matthew 22:37-40; John 3:16; Romans 8:38-39; 1 Corinthians 13:4,7-8; 14:1; Ephesians 1:6,18-19; Hebrews 8:10; 1 John 3:1; 4:14

Who I Am in Christ

I am a child of God; God is spiritually my Father.
Romans 8:14-15; Galatians 3:26; 4:6; John 1:12

I am a new creation in Christ; old things have passed away and all things have become new.
2 Corinthians 5:17

I am in Christ.
Ephesians 1:1-4; Galatians 3:26,28

I am an heir with the Father and a joint heir with Christ.
Galatians 4:6-7; Romans 8:17

I am reconciled to God and am an ambassador of reconciliation for Him.
2 Corinthians 5:18-19

I am a saint.
Ephesians 1:1; 1 Corinthians 1:2; Philippians 1:1; Colossians 1:2

I am God's workmanship, created in Christ for good works.
Ephesians 2:10

I am a citizen of heaven.
Ephesians 2:19; Philippians 3:20

I am a member of Christ's body.
1 Corinthians 12:27

I am united to the Lord and am one spirit with Him.
1 Corinthians 6:17

I am the temple of the Holy Spirit.
1 Corinthians 3:16; 6:19

I am a friend of Christ.
John 15:15

I am a slave of righteousness.
Romans 6:18

I am the righteousness of God in Christ.
2 Corinthians 5:21

I am enslaved to God.
Romans 6:22

I am chosen and ordained by Christ to bear fruit.
John 15:16

I am a prisoner of Christ.
Ephesians 3:1; 4:1

I am righteous and holy.
Ephesians 4:24

I am hidden with Christ in God.
Colossians 3:3

I am the salt of the earth.
Matthew 5:13

I am the light of the world.
Matthew 5:14

I am part of the true vine.
John 15:1-2

I am filled with the divine nature of Christ and escape the corruption that is in the world through lust.
2 Peter 1:4

I am an expression of the life of Christ.
Colossians 3:4

I am chosen of God, holy and dearly loved.
Colossians 3:12; 1 Thessalonians 1:4

I am a child of light.
1 Thessalonians 5:5

I am a partaker of a heavenly calling.
Hebrews 3:1

I am more than a conqueror through Christ.
Romans 8:37

I am a partaker with Christ and share in His life.
Hebrews 3:14

I am one of God's living stones, being built up in Christ as a spiritual house.
1 Peter 2:5

I am a chosen generation, a royal priesthood, a holy nation.
1 Peter 2:9

I am the devil's enemy.
1 Peter 5:8

I am born again by the Spirit of God.
John 3:3-6

I am an alien and stranger to this world.
1 Peter 2:11

I am a child of God who always triumphs in Christ and releases His fragrance in every place.
2 Corinthians 2:14

I am seated in heavenly places in Christ.
Ephesians 2:6

I am saved by grace.
Ephesians 2:8

I am a recipient of every spiritual blessing in the heavenly places in Christ.
Ephesians 1:3

I am redeemed by the blood of the Lamb.
Revelation 5:9

I am part of the bride of Christ and am making myself ready for Him.
Revelation 19:7

I am a true worshipper who worships the Father in spirit and in truth.
John 4:24

Blessing

I am created for blessing. As a result, I am fruitful in every good thing and I multiply and increase in blessing. Because my God has blessed me, no curse can touch me. In the name of Jesus Christ and by the power of His blood, I decree His covenant of blessing around my life and all that pertains to me.

Nothing but blessing is permitted to come into my life or sphere of influence. If the enemy attempts to attack me, he will be caught in the act and pay sevenfold what he stole and then I will plunder his house, for I only accept blessing. His attempts create testimonies of God's increased blessings in my life.

Like Abraham, I am blessed and am called to be a blessing. Through my life in Jesus, nations are blessed.

Blessings come upon me and overtake me. Blessings are attracted to me. I am a blessing magnet. I am blessed coming in and blessed going out. I am blessed in the city and blessed in the field. The heavens are open over my life and the rain of God's abundant goodness falls on my life and all that pertains to me. No good thing has He withheld from me. I am blessed in everything I put my hands to.

My household is blessed. My food is blessed. My clothing is blessed. My vehicles are blessed. My business and matters of business are blessed. My children, family, and all who labor with me and for me are blessed. My finances are blessed and my spirit, soul, and body are fully blessed, because Jesus established an eternal, unbreakable covenant of blessing for me.

I am blessed with the Kingdom of heaven and its bounty because I recognize my need of God in all things and at all times. I am blessed with comfort when I mourn. I am always blessed with a satisfied heart because I hunger and thirst for righteousness. I am blessed with mercy because I show mercy to others. I am blessed with insights and visitations from God because I am pure in spirit.

I am called a son/daughter of God because I am a peacemaker. When I am persecuted for the sake of righteousness or when people insult me and speak lies about me, I am blessed with heavenly and eternal reward. I am blessed because I hear the Lord's Word and act on it. I am a doer of the Word and not a hearer only.

Because I love wisdom and righteousness I am blessed and my dwelling is blessed. The blessing of the Lord has made me rich and He adds no sorrow to it. Because I trust in the Lord I am blessed. I am blessed with every spiritual blessing in the heavenly places in Christ. Grace and peace are multiplied unto me in the knowledge of Christ.

I have been granted everything that pertains to life and to godliness. I have been given all the magnificent promises in the Word of God. I sow blessings bountifully and therefore I reap blessings bountifully. I always look for ways I can bless others. The Lord blesses me, indeed, and enlarges my realms of influence. His hand of grace and blessing is with me, and He keeps me from harm. I am truly blessed in all things, for my Father in heaven has chosen gladly to give me the Kingdom.

My God blesses me continuously and causes His face to shine upon me. He is gracious unto me and grants me peace.

Scriptural References:
Genesis 1:28; 12:2; Deuteronomy 28:1-13; Numbers 6:22-27; Proverbs 3:13,33; 6:31; 10:6; 10:22; 16:20; Matthew 5:3-11; Luke 11:28; 12:32; Ephesians 1:3; 2 Peter 1:2-4; James 1:22; 1 Chronicles 4:10

Favor

*I*n Christ Jesus, I am favored by my heavenly Father. The favor He has given His Son has been given to me. This is undeserved, unmerited favor that is granted me in Christ. His favor is a free gift to me, for which I am very thankful. As Jesus kept increasing in wisdom and stature, and in favor with God and men, so also do I, because I abide in Jesus and He abides in me.

I embrace the favor of God, for it is better than silver and gold. The favor of God on my life endures for a lifetime and causes my mountain of influence and blessing to stand strong. His favor surrounds me like a shield against my enemies.

The Lord favors me with vindication and delights in my prosperity. His blessing on my life attracts the rich among the people who seek my favor.

By the favor of the Lord, the works of my hands are confirmed and established. All that I put my hands to is favored. My steps are bathed in butter and the rock pours out oil for me. As I seek the Lord's favor, He is gracious unto me according to His Word. I am favored in my home and favored in the workplace. I am favored everywhere I go and in all that I do.

I love wisdom and seek diligently for wisdom and understanding. Therefore I have been granted favor by the Lord and am favored by others. In the light of my King's face is life, and His favor is like a cloud with the spring rain over me. His favor is like heavenly dew that falls on my life.

I am favored in His presence and He goes before me revealing His goodness and glory to me. His favor opens doors of opportunity for me that no man can shut. By His favor I have been granted the keys of the Kingdom and whatever I bind on earth is bound in heaven. Whatever I loose on earth has been loosed in heaven. His righteous scepter of favor is extended towards me. Whatever I ask in the name of Christ He grants unto me when I make my requests and petitions according to His will. He daily grants me great favor because of the covenant blood of Christ and the promises in His Word.

Blessed be the Lord who favors His people!

Scriptural References:
Exodus 33:13-19; Esther 5:2; Job 29:6; Psalm 5:12; 30:5,7; 45:6,12; 90:17; 119:58; Proverbs 8:35; 11:27; 16:15; 19:12; 22:1; Isaiah 45:1; Luke 2:52; John 15:7 17:22

Victory

I am a child of the living God. I am an heir of God and a joint heir with Jesus Christ. I am a new creation in Jesus and old things have passed away and all things have become new. I am a chosen generation, a royal priesthood, a holy nation.

I am not under guilt or condemnation. I refuse discouragement because it is not of God. God is the God of all encouragement. There is therefore now no condemnation for those who are in Christ Jesus. The law of the Spirit of life in Christ Jesus has set me free from the law of sin and death. I do not listen to Satan's accusations, for he is a liar, the father of lies. I gird up my loins with truth. Sin does not have dominion over me.

I flee from temptation, but if I do sin I have an advocate with the Father who is Jesus Christ. I confess my sins and forsake them. God is faithful and just to forgive me, cleansing me from all unrighteousness. I am cleansed by the blood of the Lamb. I am an overcomer because of the blood of Jesus and because of the word of my testimony.

No weapon that is formed against me shall prosper and I shall confute every tongue that rises up against me in judgment. My mind is renewed by the Word of God.

The weapons of my warfare are not carnal but mighty through God to the pulling down of strongholds; I cast down imaginations and every high thing that exalts itself against the knowledge of Christ. I bring every thought captive into obedience to the truth.

I am accepted in the Beloved. Greater is He that is in me than he that is in the world. Nothing can separate me from the love of God which is in Christ Jesus my Lord. I am the righteousness of God in Christ Jesus. I am not the slave of sin but of righteousness. I continue in His Word. I know the truth and the truth sets me free. Because Christ has set me free, I am free indeed. I have been delivered out of the domain of darkness and am now abiding in the Kingdom of God.

I am not intimidated by the enemy's lies. He is defeated. For this purpose Christ came into the world, to destroy the works of the evil one. I submit to God and resist the devil. The enemy flees from me in terror because the Lord lives mightily in me. I give the devil no opportunity. I give no place to fear in my life. God has not given me a spirit of fear but of love, of power and of a sound mind. Terror shall not come near me because the Lord is the strength of my life and He always causes me to triumph in Christ Jesus.

In Christ, I am the head and not the tail. I am above and not beneath. A thousand shall fall at my side and ten thousand at my right hand, and none shall touch me. I am seated with Christ in the heavenly places far above all principalities and powers. I have been given power to tread upon serpents, scorpions and over all the power of the enemy. Nothing shall injure me. No longer will the enemy oppress me. I defeat him by the authority that Christ has given me. I am more than a conqueror through Christ.

Scriptural References:
Deuteronomy 28:13; Psalm 27:1; 91:7; Isaiah 54:17; Luke 10:19; John 8:36,44; Romans 6:16; 8:1-2,17,32,37,39; 12:2; 2 Corinthians 2:14; 5:17,21; 10:3-5; Ephesians 1:6,20-21; 4:27; 6:14; Colossians 1:13; 2 Timothy 1:7; James 4:7; 1 Peter 2:9; 1 John 1:9; 2:1; 3:8; Revelation 12:11

Wisdom

*J*esus Christ has become wisdom, righteousness, sanctification and redemption unto me. Because Christ dwells within me, I know wisdom and instruction. My God gives unto me a spirit of wisdom and of revelation in the knowledge of Christ. When I lack wisdom, I ask in faith and it is given to me generously. This is heavenly wisdom which is first pure, then peaceable, gentle, easily entreated, full of mercy and good fruits, unwavering and without hypocrisy.

I discern the sayings of understanding and I receive instruction in wise behavior, justice and fairness. I walk in the fear of the Lord which is the beginning of knowledge. Jesus pours out His spirit of wisdom upon me and makes His words of wisdom known to me.

I receive the sayings of wisdom and I treasure the commandments of the Lord within me. My ear is attentive to wisdom and I incline my heart to understanding. I cry for discernment and lift my voice for understanding.

I seek for wisdom as for silver and search for it as for hidden treasures. Because of this I will discern the fear of the Lord and discover the knowledge of God. The Lord gives me wisdom.

From His mouth comes knowledge and understanding. He stores up sound wisdom for me. He is a shield to me. He guards my paths with justice and preserves my way. Wisdom enters my heart and knowledge is pleasant to my soul. Discretion guards me and understanding watches over me to deliver me from the way of evil.

I do not let kindness and truth leave me. I bind them around my neck and write them on the tablet of my heart so that I find favor and good repute with God and man. I trust in the Lord with all my heart and I do not lean on my own understanding. In all my ways I acknowledge Him and He makes my paths straight. I am blessed because I find wisdom and I gain understanding.

I have a long, full life because it is in wisdom's right hand, and I have the riches and honor that are in wisdom's left hand. Because I love wisdom, all my paths are peace and my ways pleasant. Wisdom is a tree of life to me and I am blessed because I hold her fast. I inherit honor because of my love for wisdom, and my dwelling is blessed.

I acquire wisdom and understanding. I do not forsake wisdom; therefore, wisdom is my guard. I love wisdom and am watched over. Because I prize and embrace wisdom, wisdom exalts and honors me. Wisdom places a garland of grace on my head and presents me with a crown of beauty. I call wisdom my sister and understanding my intimate friend.

Because I love wisdom, both riches and honor are with me, enduring wealth and righteousness. Wisdom endows me with wealth and fills my treasuries. I listen to wisdom and daily watch at her gates. I eat wisdom's food and drink of the wine that she has mixed. I forsake folly and live. I proceed in the way of understanding. When I speak, I speak noble things, and the opening of my mouth produces right things. My mouth utters truth. All the utterances of my mouth are in righteousness because I walk in the way of wisdom.

Scriptural References:
Proverbs 1:2-3,7,23; 2:1-12; 4:5-9; 7:4; 8:6-8; 9:5-6; 1 Corinthians 1:30; Ephesians 1:17; James 1:5; 3:17

Glory

*I*n Christ I am filled with and have access to the same glory the Father gave to His Son. Jesus is a shield to me each and every day. He is the glory and the lifter of my head.

Jesus is the King of glory and He lives powerfully in me because I open up the gates of my heart and life to Him. He is the Lord of hosts who is strong and mighty. He is mighty in all my battles. Jesus, the King of glory, prevails over all my enemies. His glory is my rear guard and my back is always covered. When I am persecuted for the sake of righteousness, I am greatly rewarded because the spirit of glory and of God rests upon me. In Christ, I inherit the throne of glory. I am seated with Him in the heavenly places far above all demonic forces and dominions.

The fire of the Lord surrounds me and He is glory in the midst of me. The glory of His presence goes before me at all times and gives me rest. His glory is manifest in

His great goodness that visits my life each day. I decree, "The Lord is good and His lovingkindness endures forever! The Lord is good and His lovingkindness endures forever!" As I make this sure confession, the glory of the Lord fills my body, His temple, afresh.

I arise and shine because Jesus, my Light, has come, and the glory of the Lord has risen upon me. In the midst of great darkness that covers the earth, the glory appears upon me. Nations and kings come to the brightness of my rising.

I have access to the wealth, gold and silver in the earth as a result of the glory of Christ that is in me and on me. All the gold and all the silver is His. All the earth and its fullness belong to Him and all that is His has been given to me in Christ. I exercise my faith to receive the fullness of His glory and, as a result, the latter glory of the house (my life) is greater than the former.

All my needs are met according to His riches in glory by Christ Jesus. The knowledge of His glory – the glory of His salvation, healing, deliverance, provision, strength, signs and wonders, and presence – fills the earth as the waters cover the sea. The Lord's works appear to me and His glory to my children.

Glory and honor are in His presence. Strength and gladness are in His place. I imbibe of His goodness each and every day and declare His glory and marvelous works.

Be exalted, O God, above the heavens. Let your glory be above all the earth. In You my salvation and glory rest. Blessed be the name of the Lord forever, and may the whole earth be filled with Your glory. Amen and Amen.

Scriptural References:

Exodus 33:14-19; 1 Samuel 2:8; 1 Chronicles 16:24,27; Psalm 3:3; 24:1,7-10; 57:11; 62:7; 72:19; 90:16; 96:3; Isaiah 58:8; 60:1-3,5,9; Habakkuk 2:14; Haggai 2:8-9; Zechariah 2:5; John 17:22; Ephesians 1:20-22, 2:6; Philippians 4:19; 1 Peter 4:14

Provision and Resource

I seek first the Kingdom of God and His righteousness, and all the things that I need are added unto me, for my heavenly Father knows what I need even before I ask. I do not fear, for it is my Father's good pleasure to give me the Kingdom.

I acknowledge that all my needs are met according to God's riches in glory by Christ Jesus. Grace and peace are multiplied unto me through the knowledge of God and of Jesus my Lord. His divine power has given me all things that pertain unto life and godliness, through the knowledge of Him who has called me to glory and virtue. Blessed be the God and Father of my Lord Jesus Christ, who has blessed me with every spiritual blessing in the heavenly places in Christ. The Lord is a sun and a shield to me and will give me grace and glory. No good thing will He withhold from me as I walk uprightly.

I choose to sow bountifully, therefore I will reap bountifully. I give to the Lord, to His people, and to the needy as I purpose in my heart to give. I do not give grudgingly or out of compulsion, for my God loves a cheerful giver. God makes all grace abound towards me, that I always have enough for all things so that I may abound unto every good work.

The Lord supplies seed for me to sow and bread for my food. He also supplies and multiplies my seed for sowing, and He increases the fruits of my righteousness. I am enriched in everything unto great abundance, which brings much thanksgiving to God.

I bring all my tithes into the Lord's storehouse so that there is meat in His house. As a result, He opens up the windows of heaven and pours out a blessing for me so that there is not room enough to contain it. He rebukes the devourer for my sake, so that he does not destroy the fruits of my ground and neither does my vine cast its grapes before the time. All the nations shall call me blessed for I shall have a delightful life. I am blessed because I consider the poor. Because I give freely to the poor, I will never want. My righteousness endures forever.

I remember the Lord my God, for it is He who gives me the power to make wealth, that He may confirm His covenant. Because Jesus Christ, my Savior, diligently listened to the voice of God and obeyed all the commandments, the Lord will set me high above all the nations of the earth, and all the blessings in the Kingdom shall come upon me and overtake me. Christ became poor so that through His poverty I might become rich.

The Lord increases me a thousand-fold more than I am, and blesses me just as He has promised. He prospers everything I put my hand to. I abound in prosperity. The Lord empowers me to work provisional miracles in His name. I witness miracles of multiplication, debt cancellation, and increase. Jesus came so that I would have life in its abundance. I am very blessed and favored of God and have been called to be a blessing to others.

Scriptural References

Genesis 12:2; Deuteronomy 1:11; 8:18; 28:1-2, 11-12; 1 Kings 17:9-16; 2 Kings 4:1-7; Psalm 41:1; 84:11; 112:1,9; Proverbs 28:27; Malachi 3:8-12; Matthew 6:33; Mark 6:33-44; Luke 12:32; John 10:10; 2 Corinthians 8:9; 9:6-11; Ephesians 1:3; Philippians 4:19; 2 Peter 1:2-3

Christian Character

I am the light of the world. A city set on a hill cannot be hid. I let my light so shine before men that they may see my good works and glorify my Father which is in heaven. Grace and peace are multiplied to me through the knowledge of God and of Jesus my Lord. His divine power has granted me everything that pertains to life and to godliness.

He has given me exceeding great and precious promises. I live by these promises so that I might be a partaker of His divine nature, having escaped the corruption that is in the world through lust. Besides this, I give all diligence and add to my faith virtue, and to virtue knowledge and to knowledge temperance, and to temperance patience, and to patience godliness. To godliness I add brotherly kindness and to brotherly kindness love. As these things are in me and abounding, I shall never be barren nor unfruitful in the knowledge of my Lord Jesus.

I choose to walk worthy of the Lord in every respect, being fruitful in every good work and increasing in the knowledge of God. I give thanks to my heavenly Father who has made me to be a partaker of the inheritance of the saints in light. He has delivered me from the power of darkness and has translated me to the Kingdom of His dear Son in whom I have redemption through His blood, even the forgiveness of sin.

I am an imitator of God as a dear child. I walk in love. Covetousness, fornication and all uncleanness have no part in my life, neither filthiness nor coarse jesting, nor foolish talking, which are not fitting, but rather the giving of thanks. I let no corrupt communication proceed out of my mouth, but only that which is good to the use of edifying, that it may minister grace to the hearers. I will not grieve the Holy Spirit of God whereby I have been sealed unto the day of redemption.

I choose to walk in lowliness of mind and esteem others as better than myself. I look not to my own interests but also to the interests of others. I make myself of no reputation and take the form of a bondservant.

I wait for the Lord and let integrity and uprightness preserve me. Jesus is a buckler to me because I walk uprightly. I dwell on those things that are true and honorable, whatever is right, whatever is pure, whatever is lovely, whatever is of good repute and anything that is excellent and worthy of praise.

As a child of God, I am thoroughly furnished for every good work. I consider how to provoke others to love. I put on a heart of compassion, kindness, humility, gentleness and patience. I am God's workmanship, created in Christ Jesus for good deeds which God prepared beforehand that I should walk in them.

I am patient and kind. I am not jealous. I do not brag and I am not arrogant. I do not act unbecomingly and do not seek my own way. I am not easily provoked and do not take into account a wrong suffered. I do not rejoice in unrighteousness, but rejoice with the truth. I bear all things, believe all things, hope all things and endure all things. The love of Jesus in me does not fail.

Scriptural References:
Matthew 5:14-16; 1 Corinthians 13:4-8; Ephesians 2:10; 4:29-30; 5:1-5; Philippians 2:3-7; 4:8; Colossians 1:9-14; 3:12; 2 Peter 1:2-8; Hebrews 10:24; 2 Timothy 3:17

Spiritual Strength

I am strong in the Lord and in the strength of His might. I put on the full armor of God. In Christ I can do all things because He strengthens me.

The Lord is my strength and my shield; my heart trusts in Him, and I am helped; therefore my heart exults and with my song I shall thank Him. He is my strength and my saving defense in time of trouble. The grace of the Lord Jesus Christ is with my spirit.

I build myself up in my holy faith, praying in the Holy Spirit. As I do this, I keep myself strong in the love of God. My God keeps me from falling and presents me faultless and blameless in the presence of my heavenly Father with exceeding great joy.

My help comes from the Lord who made heaven and earth. He will not allow my foot to slip and He who keeps me will not slumber. The Lord is my keeper. The Lord is my shade on my right hand. The sun does not smite me by day nor the moon by night. The Lord protects me from all evil. He keeps my soul and He guards my going out and my coming in from this time forth and forever.

When I pass through the valley of weeping, the Lord makes it a spring for me. I go from strength to strength in the Lord. The Lord God is a sun and a shield to me. He gives me grace and glory, and no good thing does He withhold from me. I am blessed because I trust in Him.

My heavenly Father grants unto me according to the riches of His glory the ability to be strengthened with power through His Spirit in my inner man, so that Christ may dwell in my heart through faith, and that I, being rooted and grounded in love, may be able to comprehend with all believers what is the breadth and length and height and depth and to know the love of Christ which surpasses knowledge, that I may be filled up to all the fullness of God.

I do not lose heart in doing good, for in due time I shall reap if I faint not. My eye is single, therefore my whole being is full of light. I am steadfast, immoveable, always abounding in the work of the Lord, knowing that my toil is not in vain in the Lord. God is my strong fortress and He sets me in His way.

By Him, I can run through a troop and by my God, I can leap over a wall. He is a shield because I take refuge in Him. He makes my feet like hinds' feet and sets me on my high places. He trains my hands for battle so that my arms can bend a bow of bronze. He has given me the shield of His salvation and His help and strength make me great. I pursue my enemies and destroy them because the Lord has girded me with strength for battle.

The Lord gives me strength when I am weary, and when I lack might He increases power. I wait on the Lord and renew my strength. I mount up with wings like eagles. I run and do not get tired; I walk and do not faint.

Scriptural References:
2 Samuel 22:30-40; Psalm 28:7-8; 37:39; 84:5-7,11; 121:1-8; Isaiah 40:29-31; Matthew 6:22; 1 Corinthians 15:58; Galatians 6:7-9; Ephesians 3:16-19; 6:10; Philippians 4:13,23; Jude 20-21,24

Empowered to Go

I receive power when the Holy Spirit comes upon me to be the Lord's witness even unto the uttermost parts of the earth. In Jesus' name I go into all the world to preach the gospel to every creature.

These signs follow me as I go because I believe. In the name of Jesus, I cast out devils, I speak with new tongues, I take up serpents, and if I drink any deadly poison it shall not harm me. When I lay hands on the sick they shall recover. I go forth and preach everywhere, and the Lord confirms the Word I preach with signs that follow. When I go, I go in the fullness of the blessing of the gospel of Christ.

The works that Jesus does, I do also in His name and even greater works I do because He has gone to the Father. Greater is He that is in me than he that is in the world. Jesus has given me power over all the power of the enemy. He has given me power over unclean spirits to cast them out and has enabled me to heal all manner of sickness and all manner of disease.

As I go, I will preach saying, "The kingdom of heaven is at hand." I will heal the sick, cleanse the lepers, raise the dead. I will cast out devils, because freely I have received so I will freely give. The Lord grants me boldness to speak His Word. He stretches out His hand toward me to heal, that signs and wonders may be done through the name of Jesus Christ. His Spirit has been poured out upon me and I prophesy.

All power in heaven and in earth has been given unto Jesus Christ. I will go in His name and teach all nations, baptizing them in the name of the Father, the Son and the Holy Spirit. I will teach them to observe all things that Jesus has taught me. Jesus is with me even unto the end of the world. He has called me to Himself and has given me power and authority over all devils and to cure diseases. He has sent me to preach the Kingdom of God and to heal the sick. As I go, Jesus prepares my way with His favor, for the Lord surrounds His righteous with favor as a shield. He sends His angels before me to watch over my ways and to bear me up lest I fall.

Like Jesus, I have been anointed with the Holy Spirit and with power. I go about doing good and healing all that are oppressed of the devil, for God is with me. He has anointed me to preach the gospel to the poor.

He has sent me to proclaim release to the captives and recovery of sight to the blind, to set free all who are downtrodden, and to proclaim the favorable year of the Lord.

I arise and shine because my light has come and the glory of the Lord has risen upon me. Darkness shall cover the earth and gross darkness the peoples, but the Lord has risen upon me and His glory appears upon me. Nations will come to my light in Christ and kings to the brightness of my rising.

My speech and my preaching is not with enticing words of man's wisdom. It is in the demonstration of the Spirit and of power that the faith of those I preach to should not stand on the wisdom of men but in the power of God, for the Kingdom of God is not in word but in power.

The Lord grants unto me, according to His riches in glory, to be strengthened with might by His Spirit in my inner man according to His glorious power unto all patience and longsuffering with joy. I labor according to His power that works mightily within me.

I preach not myself, but Christ Jesus as Lord, and myself as a bondservant of Christ and His body for Jesus' sake. For God, who said that "Light shall shine out of darkness," is the One who has shone in our hearts to give the light of the knowledge of the glory of God in the face of Christ. I have this treasure in an earthen vessel, that the surpassing greatness of the power may be of God and not of myself.

Now unto the King eternal, immortal, invisible, the only wise God who is able to do exceedingly, abundantly above all that I could ask or think, according to the power that works within me, be honor and glory forever and ever. AMEN

Scriptural References:
Psalm 5:12; 91:11; Isaiah 60:1-3; Matthew 10:1,7; 28:18-20; Mark 16:15-21; Luke 4:18; 10:1-2,19; John 14:12; Acts 1:8; 2:17-18; 4:29-30; 10:38; Romans 15:29; 1 Corinthians 2:4; 4:19; 2 Corinthians 4:5-6; Ephesians 3:16,20; Colossians 1:11,29; 1 Timothy 1:17; 1 John 4:4

Health and Healing

I praise the Lord with all that is within me and do not forget any of His benefits. He forgives all my sins and heals all my diseases; He redeems my life from the pit and crowns me with love and compassion. Jesus satisfies my desires with good things so that my youth is renewed like the eagle's.

The Lord brings me to health and healing. He heals me and lets me enjoy abundant peace and security. The Sun of Righteousness arises for me with healing in His wings and I go out and leap like a calf released from the stall. Jesus bore my sins in His body on the cross so that I might die to sin and live to righteousness. By His stripes I am healed. As my days are, so shall my strength be.

Jesus sent forth His Word and healed me; He rescued me from the grave. When I cry out, the Lord hears me; He delivers me from all my troubles. The Lord is close to me when I am brokenhearted and saves me when I am crushed in spirit. He has not given me a spirit of fear but of love, power and a sound mind.

At times I may have many troubles, but the Lord delivers me from them all; He protects all my bones; not one of them will be broken. I am like an olive tree flourishing in the house of God; I trust in God's unfailing love forever and ever.

When the Lord's servants lay hands on me I recover and when I am sick I call for the elders who pray over me, anointing me with oil in the name of the Lord. The prayer of faith saves me and the Lord raises me up.

The law of the spirit of life in Christ Jesus has set me free from the law of sin and death. Jesus is the resurrection and the life. Because I believe in Him, I will live for all eternity. In Christ I live and move and have my being.

Because I dwell in the shelter of the Most High and rest in the shadow of the Almighty, I will say of the Lord, "He is my refuge and my fortress, my God, in whom I trust." Surely He will save me from the fowler's snare and from the deadly pestilence. He covers me with His feathers, and under His wings I find refuge; His faithfulness is my shield and rampart. I do not fear the terror of night, nor the arrow that flies by day, nor the pestilence that stalks in the darkness, nor the plague that destroys at midday. A thousand may fall at my side, ten thousand at my right hand, but they will not come near me. I will only observe with my eyes and see the punishment of the wicked. Because I make the Most High my dwelling – even the Lord, who is my refuge – then no harm will befall me, no disaster will come near my tent. He will command His angels concerning me to guard me in all my ways; they will lift me up in their hands so I will not strike my foot against a stone. I will tread upon the lion and the cobra; I will trample the great lion and the serpent. Because I love the Lord, He will rescue and protect me from all accident, harm, sickness and disease. He is with me in trouble and delivers me. With long life He satisfies me and shows me His salvation.

Because I consider the poor, the Lord will deliver me in time of trouble. The Lord will protect me and keep me alive, and I shall be blessed upon the earth. He will not give me over to the desire of my enemies. The Lord will sustain me upon my sickbed; in my illness, He will restore me to health.

Scriptural References:
Deuteronomy 33:25; Psalm 34:17-20; 41:1-3; 52:8; 91; 103:1-3; 107:20; Jeremiah 33:6; Malachi 4:2; Mark 16:18; John 11:25-26; Romans 12:1; 2 Timothy 1:7; James 5:14-15; 1 Peter 2:24

Business, Ministry, and Workplace

*I*n my business, ministry, and workplace I am surrounded with favor as a shield. I arise and shine, for my light has come. The rich among the people entreat my favor.

In Christ I show no defect but function in intelligence in every branch of wisdom, being endowed with understanding and discerning knowledge. The Lord gives me the knowledge of witty inventions and causes me to grow in wisdom, in stature, and in favor with God and man.

In my business, ministry, and workplace, I am the head and not the tail. I am above and not beneath. The Lord commands blessings upon my business, ministry, and workplace, and every project that I put my hands to prospers. He establishes my business, ministry, and workplace as holy unto Himself.

My business, ministry, and workplace do not submit to the Babylonian/world system, but instead submit to the Kingdom of God and His righteousness. The integrity of the Lord guides me in my business. The Lord leans upon my business, ministry, and workplace with regard and makes it fruitful, multiplying its productivity.

No weapon formed against my business, ministry, and workplace prospers. Every tongue that rises up against it in judgement I condemn, and the Lord vindicates me. The Lord is a wall of fire around my business and workplace, and His glory is in the midst of it.

The Lord leads me by His presence, and He gives me rest. He makes goodness to pass before my business, ministry, and workplace. His goodness and mercy follow me all the days of my life. Peace, unity, love, integrity, honor, and servanthood are godly values that prevail in my business, ministry, and workplace.

I decree that Jesus Christ is Lord over my life, business, ministry, and workplace!

Scriptural References:
Exodus 33:14,19; Leviticus 26:9; Deuteronomy 28:1-13; Psalm 5:12; 23:6; 45:12; Proverbs 11:3; Isaiah 54:17; 60:1; Daniel 1:4; Zechariah 2:5; Revelation 18:4

Family and Children

*A*s for me and my family, we will serve the Lord. Because I believe in the Lord Jesus Christ, I shall be saved, and my entire house. Because I am a covenant child of God, my household is blessed. We have been blessed with every spiritual blessing in Christ. Blessings come upon us and overtake us.

My family, home, marriage, and children are blessed, and all that I put my hands to do. I am blessed coming in and I am blessed going out. The Lord has established my household as a people for Himself. He causes us to abound in prosperity in the offspring of our bodies, in the offspring of our beasts, and in the produce of our ground. The Lord surrounds my family and entire household with favor as a shield. No good thing does He withhold from us. His banner is love over my home, marriage, and family. No weapon formed against us as a family prospers. What the Lord has blessed, no man can curse. We abide in the shadow of the Almighty and no evil befalls us.

My children shall be mighty on the earth, for the generation of the upright are blessed. They shall be as signs and wonders in the earth.

My children will flourish like olive plants around my table. They are a gift from the Lord, and the fruit of the womb is my reward. My children are like arrows in the hand of a warrior. My sons in their youth are as grown-up plants and my daughters as corner pillars fashioned as for a palace.

Lord, Your covenant with me declares that Your Spirit which is upon me and Your words which You have put in my mouth shall not depart from my mouth, nor from the mouths of my children, nor from the mouths of my children's children. All my children shall be taught of the Lord, and great shall be their peace and prosperity. In righteousness they will be established and they will be far from oppression. They will not be led into temptation but they will know deliverance from evil.

I confess that my children are pure in heart and therefore they shall see God. They hunger and thirst after righteousness, therefore they are filled. The Spirit of the Lord is poured out upon my children and they prophesy. The Lord's blessing is upon them. They will spring up among the grass like poplars by streams of water. One will say, I am the Lord's, and another one will call on the name of Jacob; and another will write on their hand, "Belonging to the Lord."

I confess that my children are seekers of wisdom and understanding. They hold fast to Your Word and to Your ways. They treasure Your commandments and they cry for discernment. The spirit of wisdom is poured out upon my children and my children's children, and words of wisdom are being made known to them.

The Lord keeps my family from falling and presents them blameless before the presence of the Father's glory with exceeding joy.

Scriptural References:
Deuteronomy 28:1-12; Joshua 24:15; Psalm 5:12; 84:11; 91:1,10; 112:2; 127:3-4; 128:3; 144:12; Proverbs 1:23; 2:2-3; Song of Solomon 2:4; Isaiah 8:18; 44:3-5; 54:13-14,17; 59:21; Matthew 5:6,8; 6:13; Acts 2:17; 16:31; Ephesians 1:3; Jude 24

Great Grace

*G*reat grace abundantly blesses me, fills me, and empowers me each and every day. God's grace (His undeserved, unmerited favor toward me and His divine influence upon my heart and life) enables me to fulfill His will and purpose in and through my life.

The grace of the Lord Jesus Christ is at work within me both to will and to do of His good pleasure.

I am saved by grace, justified by grace, and enabled to fulfill His daily work by His amazing grace. His grace and peace are multiplied unto me as I humble myself before Him. As I increase in grace and power, I will perform wonders and signs among the people that will bring glory to God.

I have been granted grace by Christ to enable me to walk in the gifts and callings I was destined to fulfill. Jesus has invited me to come boldly before His throne of grace so that I may obtain mercy and grace to help in time of trouble. I have free access to this glorious privilege through the blood of Christ.

I am not under the law or in bondage to it, but I enjoy the grace of God who fulfilled all the law for me through Christ. I have the fulfillment of the law within me because of the finished work of the Cross. God's amazing grace has granted me everything that pertains to life and to godliness. I have done nothing to deserve this goodness and favor, as it is a gift given because of His great love for me.

I choose to live worthy of the grace of God. I allow His grace to motivate me to do His will and purposes and to enable me to bring glory to His name. God's grace teaches me to live a godly life and to deny sin. His grace grants me a heart that desires and loves righteousness. As a result, I love righteousness and hate wickedness and am anointed with the oil of joy in great measure.

The grace of my Lord Jesus Christ grants me favor and success everywhere I go and in all that I do as I follow Him. As grace has been extended toward me, I extend grace to others and therefore show them the goodness and love of God. Freely, freely, I have received, so I freely, freely give.

Today, I receive increased and multiplied measures of His amazing grace. I am forever grateful to God for

His glorious gift of amazing grace and therefore I proclaim His grace and peace to others.

Scripture References:
Matthew 10:8; John 1:16; Acts 15:11; Romans 6:7; Ephesians 1:2; 2:5-8; Philippians 2:13; 2 Timothy 1:9; Hebrews 4:16; James 4:6; 2 Peter 1:2-4

Rejuvenation

Bless the Lord, O my soul, and all that is within me, bless His holy name.

Bless the Lord, O my soul, and forget not all His benefits;

Who forgives all your (my) iniquities,

Who heals all your (my) diseases;

Who redeems your (my) life from destruction,

Who crowns you (me) with lovingkindness and tender mercies,

Who satisfies your (my) mouth with good things,

So that your (my) youth is renewed like the eagle.
—Psalm 103:1-5

*I*n Jesus' name I decree that my youth is renewed like the eagle as I am renewed in the spirit of my mind. I watch over my heart with all diligence because from it flows the issues of life. What I allow in my mind and heart affects my body and the state of my life. Therefore my body is rejuvenating daily because I am focused on the truth, goodness, and great benefits of the Lord.

I do not allow sin to enter my life, and therefore the consequence of sin (which is the spirit of death that oppresses the body and mind) has no hold on me. If I do sin, I repent and am forgiven and cleansed from all unrighteousness, guilt, condemnation, and shame because of Christ's great mercy. My body is completely free from the destructive power of sin. The law of the spirit of life in Christ Jesus has set me free from the law of sin and death. I do not allow unforgiveness, bitterness, or offense to have place in my life. Therefore, my life and body are free from these destructive contaminants.

Jesus is Life and Light. The words He speaks are spirit and life. Therefore I am filled afresh with His ageless, eternal Life and Light when I focus on Him and drink of His promises, declaring their power into my body, soul, and spirit.

In Jesus' name I call forth His Spirit, Life, and Light to fill every cell, organ, and fiber of my being. I meditate on His Spirit, Life and Light filling my mind, emotions, organs in the head, neck, chest, abdomen, back, legs, arms, feet, and hands. Come Spirit, Life and Light of Christ. Fill me. Renew me. I speak renewal through the power of Jesus into every organ of my body.

I speak to my skin (the largest organ of my body), and command rejuvenation and elasticity to be restored to every cell of it. "Skin, receive the glory of God in Jesus' name." I call forth the glory of God to arise, shine, and appear on me as Isaiah prophesied and as was seen on both Jesus and Moses.

I speak to my sight and hearing in the name of Jesus and call forth excellence and precision into these organs of my body. I command health and strength to all my bones, muscles, tendons, and joints. I decree that my heart and circulatory system are strong and healthy. My lungs and respiratory system are vibrant in Christ, functioning at optimum levels of performance. In Christ's name, I speak health and rejuvenation to all the digestive, endocrine, hormonal, immune, reproductive, nerve, electrical, and elimination organs of my body.

I care for my mind and emotions and, as a result, I think only on those things that are true, honorable, right, pure, good, lovely and all that is of good report. I am anxious for nothing because I submit to the Lord all that concerns me. I reject negative thoughts and emotions and cast all my cares upon Him because He cares for me. As a result, my body, mind, and emotions have no stress – only peace. I am kept in perfect peace because I set my mind and heart on Him. I have the mind of Christ, and my thinking processes are sharp.

My youth is renewed daily in Christ. I abide in Him and His Life flows in and through me.

When I am weary, God increases strength in me. When I lack might, He increases power. I run and do not get weary. I walk and do not faint, for the Lord renews my strength when I wait on Him. I mount up with wings like the eagle.

I always yield fruit and will be full of fresh vision all the days of my life. Like Caleb, I will still be pursuing the fulfillment of God-given destiny after 85 years of age, being full of life, energy and ability.

I soak in His presence and glory. I receive refreshment and impartation into every part of my being. Blessed be the name of the Lord who renews and rejuvenates my body, soul, and spirit daily! As my days are, so shall my strength be. I am fully satisfied in Christ all the days of my life.

Scripture References:
Exodus 34:30; Joshua 14:11; Psalm 92:14; 103:1-5; Proverbs 4:23; Isaiah 1:1-2; 26:3; 40:29-31; Matthew 17:2; John 1:9; 6:63; 7:37; 8:12; 9:5; 14:6; Romans 6:23; 8:2; 1 Corinthians 2:16; Ephesians 4:23; Philippians 4:6-8; 1 Peter 5:7

I Am Supernatural
in Christ

*I*n Jesus, I am a new creation. Through the Holy Spirit I am able to do all the works that Jesus did, and even greater works. I am a supernatural being because of my new birth in Christ. In my spirit man, I am fully righteous and made in the image and likeness of Christ. His nature and character have been given to me. His power and glory have been given to me. By Christ's amazing promises and grace, I am filled with all that He is and all that He has.

Miracles, signs and wonders follow me when I preach the good news of the Kingdom, for the Lord Himself confirms the Word I proclaim. In the glorious name of Jesus, I create light in the darkness and order in chaos by calling those things that are not as though they are. In Christ, I have power over all the works of the enemy and nothing harms me. The strongholds of sickness, disease, oppression, possession, and demonic attack are under my feet when I take dominion in Christ. I go forth in the mighty name of Jesus that is more powerful and carries more authority than any other name.

The invisible realm of the Kingdom of God has been granted to me through the eternal, unbreakable covenant that Christ made on my behalf. My heavenly Father has chosen gladly to give me the Kingdom. I have access to the throne room and the heavenly realms by faith through the blood of Christ. I enter with boldness and confidence before the throne of grace and obtain grace and mercy to help in time of need.

The eyes of my heart and understanding are opened by the Spirit of God, so that I will know the hope of my calling in Christ. The God of my Lord Jesus Christ, the Father of glory, gives me the spirit of wisdom and of revelation in the knowledge of the Godhead and opens my understanding to know the surpassing greatness of Christ's power toward me and to all who believe. These are in accordance with the working of the strength of His might. I am seated with Christ at the right hand of the Father in heavenly places, far above all rule and authority and power and dominion, and every name that is named not only in this age but also in the one to come.

Through Christ, I have come to the city of the living God, the heavenly Jerusalem, and to myriads of angels, to the general assembly and church of the firstborn who are enrolled in heaven, and to God, the Judge of all, and to the spirits of the righteous made perfect, and to Jesus, the mediator of a new covenant, and to the sprinkled blood, which speaks better than the blood of Abel.

I have received a kingdom that cannot be shaken and therefore I show gratitude by which I may offer to God an acceptable service with reverence and awe. My God is a consuming fire.

I am an eternal being, and Eternal Life dwells within me. Therefore, I am not limited to the restraints of time and distance. As the Spirit leads, I can perform supernatural acts like Jesus did, such as walking on water, walking through walls, feeding multitudes with miraculous provision, changing substance like water to wine, altering weather patterns, being lifted up off the earth, raising the dead, and working extraordinary miracles.

Angels are dispatched into divine assignments when I declare the Word of God, for they obey the voice of the Lord's Word that I speak! The words of Jesus are spirit and life. Angels ascend and descend upon me because Christ dwells in me. They are ministering spirits sent by God to help me in my mission on the earth. Even when I do not sense them or see them, they are with me to protect me and minister to me.

As a supernatural being, my senses are exercised to discern good and evil – and I choose good. I am able to see, hear, and feel the invisible Kingdom realm around me.

I am the temple of the Holy Spirit. My being is filled with glory when I remember and proclaim the goodness of God. The Lord is good and His mercy endures forever. Because Christ dwells in me, I live under the open heaven, and blessings come upon me and overtake me. I am blessed with every spiritual blessing in the heavenly places in Christ.

I am a supernatural being encountering Christ and His Kingdom. I bring glory to God through my obedience to Him and by the word of my testimony.

Scripture References:
Genesis 1:1-3; Deuteronomy 28:1-2; 2 Kings 6:15-17; 2 Chronicles 5:13-14; Psalm 91:11-13; 103:20; Matthew 8:23-27; 10:7-8; 14:22-29; Mark 6:33-44; 16:20; Luke 10:19; 12:32; John 1:51; 2:1-10; 3:16; 6:63; 10:27; 14:12; 17:22; 20:19; Acts 1:9; 19:11; Romans 4:17; 8:14; 1 Corinthians 3:16; 2 Corinthians 5:17,21; Ephesians 1:3; 1:17-20, 2:6; Philippians 2:9-10; Hebrews 1:14; 5:14; 4:16; 10:19-22; 12:22-24, 28-29; 2 Peter 1:3-4; Revelation 12:11

12 Decrees for Your Nation

*I*n Jesus' name, I decree that my nation is turning to God and is embracing the truth of His Word.

In Jesus' name, I decree that the active, holy, and powerful conviction of the Holy Spirit is visiting every individual in my nation, drawing souls into true encounter with Christ.

In Jesus' name, I decree that all who serve the nation in government positions are visited by the righteousness, truth, and justice of God, and that they live in the fullness of Christ's wisdom in all they do. I decree that any corruption in government will be exposed and dealt with in wisdom and righteousness in order for the nation to be cleansed.

In Jesus' name, I decree that the education leaders, systems, and institutions in my nation are being filled with Kingdom values, wisdom, conviction, and truth.

In Jesus' name, I decree that the body of Christ in my nation is actively walking with and serving the Lord with fullness of focus, sincerity of faith and in the demonstration of the power of the Spirit.

In Jesus' name, I decree that those who live in my nation are kept in good health and are offered excellent health services and care. I decree that all will live in the health and strength of the Lord.

In Jesus' name, I decree that the media in my nation communicates godly morals and values, and that the gospel is favored in media.

In Jesus' name, I decree that every godly business and enterprise flourishes in my nation and every corrupt business and enterprise is exposed and falls. I decree prosperity and fruitfulness in my nation as a result of godliness, in order for every individual to have all they need.

In Jesus' name, I decree that the marriages and families in my nation are blessed with love, joy, and peace and that every home is filled with the goodness of God.

In Jesus' name, I decree that the body of Christ is mobilized into the harvest fields of my nation to bring forth much fruit.

In Jesus' name, I decree that righteousness thrives in my nation in every realm of life and that lawlessness and corruption have no place.

JESUS IS LORD OVER MY NATION!

Power of Prayer

*M*y prayers are powerful. Every prayer I pray that is according to the will of God is granted to me. When I pray, I believe that I have received and I have the request that I asked of Him.

My heavenly Father answers every prayer I pray in the Name of Jesus so that my joy will be full. When I ask of my Heavenly Father, I ask in faith, with no doubting, for all things are possible to those who believe.

Scriptural References:
Mark 9:23; 11:24 ; John 15:16; 16:24; James 1:5-6; 1 John 5:14-15

My Prayer List

Date of Prayer	Request	Scripture Promise	Date Answered

Notes:

_____

_____

_____

_____

_____

_____

My Prayer List

Date of Prayer	Request	Scripture Promise	Date Answered

Notes:

_____

_____

_____

_____

_____

_____

_____

My Prayer List

Date of Prayer	Request	Scripture Promise	Date Answered

Notes:

_____

_____

_____

_____

_____

_____

My Prayer List

Date of Prayer	Request	Scripture Promise	Date Answered

Notes:

_____

_____

_____

_____

_____

_____

Personal Decrees

Personal Decrees

PATRICIA KING

Patricia King is president of XP Ministries and co-founder of XPmedia.com, Inc. She has been a pioneering voice in ministry, with over 30 years of background as a Christian minister in conference speaking, prophetic service, church leadership, and television & radio appearances. Patricia has written numerous books, produced many CDs and DVDs, hosts the TV program "Patricia King-Everlasting Love," and is the CEO of a number of businesses. Patricia's reputation in the Christian community is world-renowned.

Christian Services Association (CSA) was founded in Canada in 1973 and in the USA in 1984. It is the parent ministry of XP Ministries, a 501-C3. They are located in Maricopa, AZ and Kelowna, B.C. Patricia King and numerous team members equip the body of Christ in the gifts of the Spirit, prophetic ministry, intercession, and evangelism. CSA/XPmedia is called to spreading the gospel through media.

AUTHOR CONTACT INFORMATION

U.S. Ministry Center	**Canada Ministry Center**
P.O. Box 1017	3054 Springfield Road
Maricopa, AZ 85139	Kelowna, B.C VIX 1A5

E-mail: info@XPmedia.com
XPministries.com
XPmedia.com
XPmissions.com
Patriciaking.com

Step into the BLESSING ZONE!

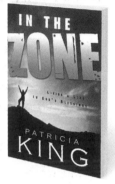

You were created to be blessed, to know the very best that God has to offer all the days of your life. If you have been living in a place of lack, hardship, or frustration, it is time to shift into the Blessing Zone and know the goodness of God in every area of your life!

In this powerful new book, Patricia King shares divine secrets of how you can step out of simply living day-to-day and live IN THE ZONE!

Unlock the Power of God in You!

Tongues presents you with keys to accelerate your growth and maturity as a believer, help you enjoy deeper intimacy with the Lord and much more! Learn: why the empowering and gifts of the Spirit are so important in our daily walk and purpose as Christians; five amazing, supernatural reasons you should pray in tongues; the role of praying in tongues in revival; how you can be baptized in the Holy Spirit and receive the gift of tongues, and much more!

Available at the "Store" at **XPmedia.com.**

Worship and Decrees that Soak You in His Purifying Presence!

The Spiritual Cleanse soaking CD is full of prayers and decrees written and proclaimed by Patricia King, accompanied by worship music from Steve Swanson. As you listen, you will be soaked in the purifying presence of the Living Word of God.

It's like taking time off and going to a "spiritual spa"! Let the power of the blood of Jesus Christ gently wash over you, as you receive a deep spiritual cleanse.

Decrees for Kids!

God's Word never returns void. It accomplishes all it is sent to do! Patricia King proclaims the words of God over your children, accompanied by worship music from Steve Swanson.

Decree for Kids! lovingly teaches children who they are in Jesus. They can listen to it while they play, on the way to school, or even while they fall asleep. Establish your children or grandchildren in the Word of the Lord so they may know His love and protection all of their lives!

Additional copies of this book and other
book titles from Patricia King and XP Publishing
are available at XPmedia.com

For Bulk/wholesale prices for stores and ministries.

Please contact: usaresource@xpmedia.com
In Canada, please contact: rcsource@xpmedia.com

Books are also available to bookstores at:
Anchor Distributors.com

www.XPpublishing.com
A Ministry of Patricia King and
XP Ministries